Written & Published by

Rakesh Sidana

I Want to Fly Where are My Wings
Copyright © RakeshSidana.Org 2015 All rights reserved. No part of this book may be reproduced in any form without permission in writing from the author, except in the case of brief quotations embodied in critical articles or reviews.

The information and insights in this book are solely the opinion of the author and should not be considered as a form of therapy advice, direction, diagnosis, and/or treatment of any kind. This information is not a substitute for medical, psychological or other professional advice, counseling or care. Neither the author not the publisher assumes any responsibility or liability whatsoever on behalf of any purchaser or reader.

Digital Printer:
Perfact Printer, Gurgaon, Haryana, India
Paperback.
ISBN: 978-1506019437

All rights reserved. Used or circulation by permission.

Dedication

This book dedicated to my mother, **Smt Mohan Devi** who worked hard to make me educated otherwise I could never FLY. She is the source of "motivational –gene" which motivates me "unconditionally" and I could achieve many heights. She will remain a source of inspiration all through my life. Also, this book is dedicated to my father **Sh. B.L.Sidana** and **everybody** who is part of my life journey.

Special Thanks To

My wife **Kriti** and two lovely daughters **Shradhaa** & **Kripa** who were less demanding during writing of this first book ;)
Shradha Sharma, **Gautam Sinha**, **Amit Grover** and **Sahiba Sethi** for writing Foreword, Introduction and Testimonials.

Ankit Jha and **Gurpreet** who helped me compiling this book and **Anuja Kumar** for final proof reading of eBook. **MeriCAR.com Team** for supporting and sponsoring this book.

All those who have faith in me even if we do not talk daily because I learnt that #**LOVE** does not need talking ;)
I love you all who thought this book will be a useful read.

My answer to "why"

This book is written to introduce "**Prachyesta - Ek Prayas**" an NGO school for underprivileged children and I am collecting donation through this book. Thank God to give me chance to help them.

I Want to Fly.
Where are My Wings

Table of Contents

Foreword………………………………………………….5

Preface……………………………………………………6

Author Introduction……………………………………11

What Others Say ………………………………………13

About NGO (Prachyesta - Ek Prayas) …………………15

1. Great business starts with Passion NOT with an idea…….16

2. Hope keeps you alive but kill your DOING………………20

3. Are you finding a reason to be UNHAPPY? ……………24

4. You have ONE and ONLY one strength…………………28

5. How to turn obstacles into OPPORTUNITIES……………32

6. What NOT to do is more IMPORTANT than what to do…34

7. You are BRAND yourself..38

8. Passion is deep rooted plant that can SURVIVE in desert..........42

9. Profitability is a PLAYGROUND. Build it................................46

10. Get Rejected, Fail FAST for Big Success...............................52

11. Hesitation is a CLOSED door in your mind..........................56

12. Speed is the key to SUCCESS..60

13. Glimpse of Success makes you run FASTER.........................62

14. Did you ACCEPT yourself yet...66

15. An Entrepreneur is a TEACHER..70

16. For success, just ensure right PEOPLE & wait for the rest.......74

About The Author...77

#Poem [I am your source. You Win. I Win]...........................79

Feedback/Testimonial Form...

* * * * *

Foreword

The best gift we have in our lives is the gift of a good book. A book in a hand is like holding learning, wisdom, mistakes and most importantly experiences. I love books, they have shaped, mentored, questioned and opened my eyes so many times. Open a book with openness of mind and heart and see the magic that begins. When Rakesh Sidana, the author of this book asked me to write a forward, i was delighted and at the same time hesitant to do it. I am delighted because a fellow entrepreneur took time to share his learning and i want to support him the best i can. Hesitant because of my lack of qualification and stature to do the book forwarding. Yet, i am doing it with joy as i loved the frankness and honesty of this book. Rakesh has poured real gems from his own experiences and observations. It's a privilege to join and learn from his experiences. Please read this book with a free mind and let the book talk to you.

SHRADHA SHARMA

Bangalore. October 2014

Shradha Sharma – Founder. YourStory.com

YourStory.com is India's no.1 media platform for entrepreneurs, dedicated to passionately championing and promoting the entrepreneurial ecosystem in India. YourStory has profiled stories of over 14,000 entrepreneurs, and has provided business networking opportunities to over 50,000 entrepreneurs via conferences. TechSparks is main annual entrepreneurship event. YourStory has representatives in Asia, Africa and USA.

Preface

We are born to fly. Everybody flies in their life. When we are born, we learn from our parents how to live a life. As we grow, we learn from people around us. We keep learning new things and growing in our professional and personal life.

"We grow. We fly"

During our life journey, we are surrounded by many obstacles and our mind remains busy solving them and we forget flying, we stop growing.

Did you realize you wanted to start your hobbies and you are still planning? Did you realize you wanted to change your job and you have not made resume yet? Did you realize that you have been planning to start your own business and you have not even made a business plan? This is what I am talking about in this book. You have stopped flying.

Who stopped you from growing? You can not blame anybody.

It's you who has not realized it. It's your mindset which has stopped showing you more options and possibilities.

You already have three wings, the ENERGY, the COURAGE and the KNOWLEDGE; you just need to use your wisdom. You have to learn new skills to achieve something big.

"You are unique and different"

Make your own path of success. You forget that you have ENERGY; you forget that you have COURAGE. You forget that you have KNOWLEDGE. You forget that your wings. Just Fly.

Let me tell you a story. Read.

In 1995, a guy was migrated from a small town to a city of opportunities. One day family stopped sending him money. He sold his room furniture and paid his room rent. No food but he had space to live. He still remembers his happiness when he got 10 bucks for 10 entries from data entry firm as a commission.

Later after more struggles, he visualized the potential of internet in India and his articles were published in The Times of India and became regular contributor to IT magazine. He appeared on TV shows for discussion on unique business model he invented.

He got d-grade in computer (almost near to fail), but he established software company. He has not seen India yet, but he did business with people all across the world.

He was not an expert programmer, but he has written code in almost every platform. He had never appeared in top-management entrance exam (CAT exam), but he has been recognized at top management institute in India (IIM-Ahmedabad).

He never had any automotive background, but his unique business model for automotive industry bringing change in the aftermarket. He has no idea how authors are made, but he has written THIS book himself.

That guy is - "me" ;)

All above events happened with courage and making strength by acquiring knowledge. I always had courage to come out of any bad situation in my life. My mind keeps thinking options and possibilities to do better. I made learning as my strength and made own success life path.

This book will tell you how above success events lead to
– an unconventional life path.

My first fly too place
when I migrated from a small town to big city.

My second fly
when my articles got featured in leading newspapers.

My third fly
when I launched my company and became my own boss.

I was growing
and FLYING.

I always wanted to build my own dot-com company around unique business idea and founded MeriCAR.com which was recognized and appreciated by everybody in India. This is the only company in India which created new business category in Automotive Industry. My company got two rounds of equity funding from reputed top investors in the country.

> By the time this book will be in your hands,
> I would have taken another fly.
> I am flying. I am living my life.

Just Fly ;)

✳ ✳ ✳ ✳

"The only ONE thing that is common amongst all entrepreneurs has been - #persistence"

This book gives you an insight into that SINGLE trait. - PERSISTENCE

Author Introduction

I met Rakesh Sidana, four years ago, when I was at a transition point in my life as I moved from being an entrepreneur to a seed investor. The first thing that hit me about him was the fact that he was a "street entrepreneur" i.e a person who is fearless and will build ground up. That first impression has not changed in the 4 years that I have known him!

His entrepreneurial journey is now 10 years old (including his last international outsourcing business) but what I always admire about him is his ability to "dream" with adversity staring at him in the face.

The book that you are holding in your hand has been written "during" the journey of being an entrepreneur. This makes it unique as it is "raw" and from the heart.

People end up writing about their entrepreneurial journey once they have reached their destination. Rakesh has written it as he is traveling along this road. He is giving you an "emotional narrative" based on incidents that are a few months/days old. It is similar to reading a person's diary with a glimpse into the mind as events unfurl.

I have always believed that the capacity to bear financial pain is what separates a great entrepreneur from a good one. Every person in the world has a financial breaking point beyond which he or she will give up on the road of creation.

Some people also define it as being persistent and if one were to look at ALL the traits that ANY successful entrepreneur has had in the world, the only ONE thing that is common amongst all has been persistence. This book gives you an insight into that SINGLE trait which is true for finding happiness not only in business but in ANY thing that you may want to do in life.

As our country is poised to make the "great" leap forward in terms of prosperity and a dramatic change in quality of life for its citizens, I am sure this book will help in its own way to show the vast majority of our people that indeed "anything is possible".

GAUTAM SINHA

Mumbai. October 2014

Gautam Sinha – Mentor, Author – Flying Business Class

A serial entrepreneur since 1996, He has started (and shut down!) two companies before successfully exiting his third venture in early 2008. He is founder of My First Cheque, a seed investment company and he was CEO of his last company TVA Allegis which is a part of Allegis Group a $6 billion recruiting and staffing company. He loves working with people, as a coach, to help create something which appears "fantastic" at the current moment. For him the journey is always as important as the destination, as he believe we only live once! so he always has fun while executing the "impossible" !
You can reach him at: http://www.gautamsinha.org

✻ ✻ ✻ ✻ ✻

What Others Say

"Every entrepreneur has a story to tell, and then there are few who have many stories to tell - that is Rakesh Sidana for you. He comes across as a passionate startup guy who is bubbling with enthusiasm every single time you meet him, but his smiling face hides many a travails he has gone through. This book highlights few important lessons for future entrepreneurs and I wish many students and startups will learn from his variety of experiences. All the best to Rakesh and family!!"

AMIT GROVER (Gurgaon)
Founder, CEO - Nurture Talent Academy

"Simple and compelling is the two word review that I would describe as I closed the last page of this exhilarating and gripping motivational book written by successful business magnet Rakesh Sidana. While most motivational books that are meant for inspiration gets lost in the ocean of jargons here is a book that comes as breath of fresh air from the world of simple language. 'I want to Fly. Where are my wings' is a book that motivates you to pick it up to read and then compels you not to put it down till the last page."

"Actually no problem is bigger than your mindset" is a shout out to anybody who is stuck in the vicious circle of doubts and problems and unable to succeed. When Rakesh Sidana talks about focus and goal setting in his book he says **'what to do and mainly what not to do'**. This concept sums up prioritizing and time management. On the parameters of simplicity and gripping, this book is a winner hands down. I would highly recommend it to all aspiring businessmen and students."

JASEENA BACKER (Kerala)
Psychologist and Author

"I want to fly. Where are my wings" Is a wonderful read for the aspiring entrepreneurs or anyone wanting to realize his/her dreams. It's a successful compilation of Rakesh Sidana's daily learning from his entrepreneurial journey, coming from a humble background with just dreams in his heart he has made it really great for others to learn and get inspired.

My message for the readers of this book will be that you're all awesome, you're the fire and you just need some petroleum (purpose) to burn and shine more in life and realize your true potential.

SAHIBA SETHI, Entrepreneur and Author, Gurgaon.

"I felt honoured and I hope I'm able to inspire you to read the book through my testimonial, the way I got inspired after reading the book. We read and hear a lot of inspirational quotes, but hardly we remember them or follow. Now, this book has beautifully compiled the required ingredients to be a successful entrepreneur in one place, i.e in the book, I hope I can fly, where are my wings.

Being a serial entrepreneur myself, I can tell you that I could correlate with the views expressed by the author, for they are honest, real time and true. When I went through the index to read the names of the chapters, I could see myself nodding my head with most of them, as if someone just clearly understands what is like being an entrepreneur.

RUNJHUN GUPTA, ZipOut Dance Academy, Noida.

✳ ✳ ✳ ✳

About NGO

Prachyesta - Ek Prayas

Rakesh Sidana is introducing "**Prachyesta - Ek Prayas**" - an Non-governmental Organisation (NGO) school for underprivileged children and collecting donation through this book.

This school is supporting and polishing the brilliance of the underprivileged children who have had no or very little access to formal schooling, an endeavor of a few ordinary citizens of the country, thinking beyond their work, home, family and children.

The school was started from a hut within a nearby slum colony in 2013 at Sector 57, Gurgaon, Haryana, India. Kids Classes are still managed in the Hut.

This school was envisaged as a bridge to support and polish the brilliance of less fortunate children who have had no access to formal schooling till now and to bring them to a level from where they could be absorbed into mainstream. The school members are residents of neighbor colonies around Sector 57 in Gurgaon, Haryana, India. NOTE: You can contribute to Prachyesta - Ek Prayas by buying print version of this book or you can also contact "Prachyesta - Ek Prayas" directly at: prachyestha.org@gmail.com

#PASSION

"Great Business starts

*with #**Passion***

NOT with

just an idea"

Passion is something which makes you work wholeheartedly. And your body, your mind, your brain all support one purpose, the idea..

Any unique idea which comes to your mind is an outcome of brain based on information collected in your subconscious mind. Your mind finds solid and relevant reasons to EXPLORE that idea, even if that idea looks stupid to follow, but passion is the driver.

Assume that Passion is YOU, and idea is a BOOK. You want to keep reading a book and love to read this book on the subject. You enjoy reading the book and never get tired. The pages of book are so many (100000000000 book pages... ha ha ;) that it will never finish in this life. Why idea is like a book, because you keep exploring more and more. Assume you get another book and you love it too, then you keep reading it. So, passion is something to FOLLOW patiently and keep enjoying it.

If you don't enjoy it and get tired easily, you are not Passionate about it.

There are many businesses, but you choose one idea to work upon and build business out of it. The starting point is – The Passion. You have to ask yourself, if that idea keeps you glued and you enjoy exploring it. You must enjoy an idea.

Obsession is WITHOUT a Purpose.
Passion is with a Purpose.

During my college and university days, I had passion for painting; I could be without meals for long if I was working on a large canvas painting. I painted many artworks, participated displaying art galleries, gifting art to college, friends. Even I couldn't make it profession, but that was passion to create excellent artwork. Creating an ART was the OUTCOME. People liked it.

In 1995, I shifted to Delhi. Internet technology was another idea to explore. I explored it so much that the leading newspaper published my articles because I gathered considerable amount of KNOWLEDGE around those technologies. I wrote about my research and knowledge everywhere I got chance. Since I liked exploring something which didn't exist, that becomes passion. Passion is love.

Later in 2008, I built a unique business in India. When I started exploring it, many people told me that it will not work. Many! I have no count. Did I stop it? No. Not at all.

I explored it in a length that people published my article. I was on TV shows and featured in the leading newspaper again and have been recognized with "Unusual Successful Startup" in India (Source: The Economic Times).

Exploring, Researching is a Passion.

For better success, your idea must be driven by passion or you have to change the idea. If you are working on an idea just for sake of EARNING, there are less chances you can drive it for long. Earning should never be a starting point for passion driven businesses. You must expect earning after building the business from that idea by creating huge "value" for the industry.

Did you know that all investors (who invest into startups) look for entrepreneurs with passion as pre-requisite qualification? Yes. Because they love their MONEY so much that they don't want to give it to somebody who can not chase something passionately and run away with their money ;)

This is the reason, everybody say – Be Yourself. When you want to do what you love to do, automatically you are matching your likeable idea with your passion (the love).

Passion is a life being in #LOVE.

#HOPE

#Hope

keeps you alive but

but kill your DOING.

Never STOP

doing"

When you start hoping, you start living a positive life. For mind, hope is basically a "positive" DREAM which has not come true yet.

The day you will stop hoping, the extreme negativity will infect your mind and might kill you, so hope keeps you alive. You can spend whole life with HOPE.

Like everything has pros and cons, hope has side affects. You will stop DOING with a hope that the expected thing will happen. You pray, you stay idle; you sit down, take rest and assume it will happen. No. Not at all. You still have to keep working, doing, struggling, chasing your goal, changing business models, changing ideas, changing career jobs till you reach there where you want to reach.

"Efforts will make you WIN, not just hope"

Here is a list of activities you must do to avoid "hope-side-effects"

1. Remind Yourself the Ultimate Goal Again and Again

How many times I have reminded that i have 50 more articles to write before it becomes 100. I am writing more and more articles even when nobody is reading it with some hope... Ha ha ;)

Like above example, when you remind a goal, you get more energy and mind works for you to give you more possibilities, more options.

Even if you have many hopes, but you must have to visualize where you are now. Even if you get stuck somewhere, few things may not be working, but you must know where is your destination. Your career goal. Your purpose of this life.

If you don't have any goal, please keep hope, you can still live your life. Hope has a power. At the age of 70, you can write a book titled - "my hopes which never happened"... Ha ha ;)

2. Find more possibilities

There are options which you may have not tried yet. More business ideas, more tasks, more career options. Get advice. Find different ways to achieve what you want.

3. Start doing different things

There are possibilities; you still need to re-think on something which has not been achieved yet. Take a gap, but don't stop doing. Do anything, but don't sit idle. Apply to hobbies classes while you are still searching for a job. Write a blog while you are planning to start your own company. Write a book if you have just pivoted the business model and have enough time to see that scaling. You will get new energy, learn new skills. Take job leaves, but don't stop "doing". Start different path, but NEVER stop doing.

Start Living on "DOING", not on hopes

✳ ✳ ✳ ✳ ✳

#HAPPINESS

*"Are you finding a reason to be #**Unhappy**. You don't need a REASON to be happy."*

Be Happy ;)

Human is an emotional entity on this earth and it needs few things to satisfy its emotional needs. Mind is your best "wish" friend, it plays according to you. If you need a reason to be happy, it brings it before you and you are happy. You want to be sad, your mind searches plethora of information stored in your subconscious mind and bring it in your plate and you become SAD, what a player... ha ha ;)

Win over your mind.

Now how you can be happy all the time. FUN. FUN. FUN.

Did you ever make fun of yourself?

Did you ever laugh on your own mistakes?

That fun I am talking about.

Here are few suggestions how you can play with mind.

1. Train your mind to think positive

Even if you have any bad situation, think positive. Take a gap. Change the place. Talk to different people and read good books. Think beyond the situation and mind can not play negative anymore, because you are not giving chance to your mind to search any reason. You are smarter than your mind ;)

2. Try to find opportunities in every situation

Mind will really help you to find opportunities if you put it into that direction. It will show you few possibilities from the situation which you may have not even thought yet.

✳ ✳ ✳ ✳

#STRENGTH

#STARTUP

"Your #*startup* has ONE and ONLY one #*strength*. Find it. Build it"

You got an idea, you have your new startup. Congratulations! You have chosen a new life path. In early days of starting up, your mind is filled with highly positive ENERGY and enthusiasm. The world looks so beautiful because you have just taken a new FLY. Since you are doing EVERYTHING in such an enthusiastic way and utmost joy that you sometime ignore what is your strength.

You have freedom to do what you want to do. You are your own boss. What a relief from a life you had before starting up. You are doing sales, you are doing coding, you are doing meetings, hiring and everything which you knew but didn't try or were not allowed to do. It's obvious that you have to take part in all components of your startup business but you still find what your one strength is.

Your strength means your startup strength. You have to FIND and search what you LOVE and PERFORM better than other.

Is it marketing?

Is it writing?

Is it recruitment, technical or programming? What? FIND it.

My Rule of Thumb:

Your strength must contribute 70% to your startup (your knowledge and your skills, your mentorship) and hire people for 30% with other skills.

Note: if you want to reverse my thumb rule (30% yours), you still run your startup, but it will look like this – "a shoe maker is trying to build food company" ha ha ;)

How to Find Strength of Your Startup

1. Check your PERFORMANCE and past results

The skills in which you outperform, that is core strength. Here are few skills you always think you are the best – making a best team, networking, hiring, managing people, but actually they are NOT everybody's cup of tea.

If you write good articles, which gets hits and brings revenue, better keep doing it. Hire people for marketing and technical or other areas. Don't do everything yourself. You can judge it better.

2. Draw the CORE vision

Your Vision is utmost IMPORTANT on this earth and in THIS life. Try to draw your vision which can be achieved in next 5 years or 15 years. What your company wants to be. You need to draw what capabilities you have to do to achieve that vision.

Don't hesitate to hire intelligent people at top position

You remain as visionary and founder or mentor to lead the team.

3. Be the leader

Support your team to let them explore their capabilities and compare yourself with your team's performance. Startup is a mixture of many capabilities of team members. They can tell you what your startup can become using their skills.

4. Find Mentor

When you are confused and find it difficult to get right feedback of what you can do and what you can not. Find mentor, teacher, guru who may help you.

Once I thought I can't sell, but my mentor told me I should be the only ONE who can do the BEST sales because I was perfect in explaining my clients about my vision. Last 6 years, I sold different products to the SAME clients. Retaining clients is not an easy job. The power of being visionary ;)

Know your strength. Find it FAST.

Live Your Dream. Don't waste your life ;)

Build your startup around your strength.

#OPPORTUNITIES

"For success,

turn obstacles

*into **#opportunities**.*

Not easy,

but possible"

Obstacles are part of everybody's life journey. Everybody thinks he has bigger problem than others.

Actually no problem is bigger than your mindset ;)

Opportunities are everywhere. But darkness of obstacles has made you blind. To be successful, try to see beyond the obstacles. Turn obstacles into opportunities. Obstacles are HINTS and triggers to tell you something. There are hidden gems in obstacles. These are opportunities in obstacles. You have to SEARCH them.

Why we can't see opportunities even if they are around?

Here are some reasons

1. Obstacles generate negative energy that dominates your mind. Rejections, criticism and de-motivation are obstacles to your mind. Even the world looks same, but mind sees it different.

2. Obstacles are illusions of closed doors. You don't see any help around.

3. Your hesitation cause blockage when you don't ask for help. Taking advice seems to be breaking of large hard rock door of EGO.

How to turn obstacles into opportunities

1. Focus on solutions, not on problem

Few solutions may not solve the problem exactly, but it has "side impact", yes, IMPACT. Another benefit. Solutions are options and possibilities. List down SOLUTIONS.

2. Great Opportunities are by-products of situations

It has been seen often that you were failing in something again and again, but didn't realize you have made success in something else. You can realize in every situation that you did "THIS" always correct but did "THAT" always wrong.

What you do flawlessly that becomes your STRENGTH.

In my case, writing this book is a by-product of situation when I want to use my free time. I realized i was doing well when I have written over 15000 words in a very short period of time on my personal blog (rakeshsidana.org) and have many followers and this book after blog.

In above example, killing free time is a problem. Writing a blog is an opportunity. Now I see "writing" is my skill. I am educating my company partners all across India. It has become my strength.

3. Be calm and focus on PRESENT, Not on PAST

Mind really tries to take you into your past. It has a reason. Mind has been storing every bit of past events. How problem has generated, its history and last month, last year, last 5 years, last LIFE? Oh.. I went back to previous life.. ha ha ;) Don't go into past.

Focus on solutions or possibilities or tools you have NOW!

4. Have Fun

With every solution, you can find something interesting. Possibly a new way of making your product or new technique or just a NEW MANUAL to resolve any problem. Hmmm…Just look at that paper how you have defined the problem… you are good at diagram…rough diagram with arrows, more arrows…. lines.. that crossing lines…Idea!!!!! why not make this diagram as your logo.. its too customized one. Your rough sketch become your company logo. Crazy ha ha ;) I am crazy trying to find anything while solving a problem. Have Fun while you are searching for opportunities.

Be open. Find opportunities. Be successful.

#PERFORMANCE

*"For best **#Performance**, what NOT to do is more IMPORTANT than what to do"*

It is very common when we start any new project, task and work, we try to write down every task to finish to bring best results. We focus on what to do. What more to do. More and more tasks. Mind goes into one direction because of many possibilities. But actually the best RESULT lies with finding out what NOT to do.

Yes, listing down what I should NOT do is more important than what I should do.

Why? Here is a list of reasons:

Too much excitement loses your focus.

I remain excited too much to write on every topic, but I don't find time to finish any topic, all are pending to write. I get excited so much that I write too fast on my tablet and find many spelling mistakes later.

Yes, Excitement distracts your focus.

When you are excited, mind is full of positive energy, it is too much energy and hence flows out. Things look easy to achieve. All disturb the purpose, the objective and confuse more. You find every possible opportunity as destination.

Make a list. Decide what you should NOT do.

More options. More confusion

Plethora of options make you lose your focus when every option looks doable without knowing where it will take you to. You ask too many people, everybody may give you NEW option to try.

Free Advice is everywhere around. Very common saying "why not you try this"...Free advice... ha ha ;) You are trying every option. You have got locked in your mind.

In my case, I started my company (MeriCAR.com) in niche market – car aftermarket. Did I loose the focus when everybody said it will not work? No. Today my company is the ONLY focused business into After-Sales-Service Car Market to have STRONG presence in India. We don't even sell cars, we only help people for car servicing and repairs. Making expertise from one thing is easier than from many.

Here are some points to do.

1. Don't follow other's dream.

Follow your dream. Make your own vision. If you don't visualize the ultimate goal, better you don't start it. You may be the best follower, but not great Visualizer. Think what you want to build after 10 years from now. You will never loose the focus if you know the finish line.

2. Don't work on every option

Work on only 3 best options, consider rest as JUNK

Use your own Judgment what are the best options.
Use your GUT feelings.

3. Don't ask everybody

Read other similar ideas but use your own mind. There are number of articles, blogs, interviews, videos about your business or your career and your ideas. Never forget, what you are thinking now, somebody might have already thought and shared somewhere on the internet. SEARCH it and Study.

4. Don't rely on other's STRENGTH

Know your strength. Not everything is your cup of tea. Others, your competitor or somebody in the same industry, they may be good at marketing, you may be good at technology. You decide what YOU can do better.

Start making a list of "do not do this" and then make what you should do and be successful.

#BRAND

> *"You are a **#brand** yourself,*
>
> *It's great asset.*
>
> *Build it"*

Human mind recalls information in the form of IMAGES better than data. You have images of PAST events. Memory is full of images. If one image is recalled again and again, it is hard coded into your memory. Brand is creation of hard coded memory in human mind. People's experience gets attached to Brand. Brands become assets when people remember it and start using it. Only trusted brands can survive because people's mind get refreshed with their "pleasing" memory.

Here are some of important points that will help you to build YOU as brand.

1. Focus

One Word. One Image. This is called focus. Create one service or one product, you have to build your entire world around it. Let people recall your product with one name (keyword). Close your eyes and think one product, you will see IMAGE of that brand. You can dilute products or service value if you have multiple purposes or uses or benefits. Focus on ONE value.

My venture has only ONE Focus and made a great positioning in the car aftermarket and I never tried selling "shoes" or "food" online yet. ha ha ;)

2. Story

Do you have a story behind your service, product or your company? The story which tells how did you do that to make it success. How your product look like in the initial days. How it is started. Media, blogger, interviewers will find you and want to write about your product or service. People relate three things – your brand, your service and your story. Memory needs connections. There are veins in your brain connecting each other.

I never arranged any PR media company or anybody but my interviews are published on many sites and I was on the cover of leading newspaper, also got a chance to appear on TV shows. Why? I always have a story to tell.

3. Experience. Processes

People must get the SAME experience or same process when they interact with your brand. Experience is like a FEEL. Visual must be designed to give same feel every time. CLICK on Google Search Result is NOT a feel but LIKE on facebook is a feel. If you are relying on "click model" to generate traffic on your website, chances are less that you are even near to branding stuff. You can earn from site traffic, but that is short term asset until Google keeps showing you in the search result. Brands are visuals. Experience.

4. YOU

Yes, you. I am talking about YOU as brand. Human still like humans, even we are trying to build or become Robots ha ha ;)

If you are founder of your company, you must promote your company brand. Get some "selfies" with your company product and service, that is fourth connection after focus, story and experience.

You can become brand if you meet any of the following criteria
– You love people, people love you.
– You have passion, you love what you are doing.
–   You are honest and fair.

People still love you, even if you have learnt from mistakes as nobody is perfect in this world. Why you? Because you can explain your vision better than anybody else in the world. You are the one who is passionate about your services.

World wants to listen from YOU. Speak up.

* * * * *

#PERSISTENCE

*"#**Passion** is deep rooted plant that can SURVIVE even in desert"*

Many stories are written about people who dropped out of college and have built a large organizations. How academically failed or dropped out can be successful? The passion. Yes. The passion makes them successful.

Passionate people know persistence well and they NEVER give up.

They make success from their knowledge in one particular subject or Industry category. They find it irrelevant to pursue academic education if that is NOT in their interest. Their INTEREST matters for them most than YOURS.

Passion is eagerness, deep desire to LEARN, LEARN and LEARN MORE. Research. Passionate people research so much that they can teach the world with their knowledge or invention.

Here are 6 inborn qualities of passionate people.

1. **Hungry for Knowledge**

They are hungry for knowledge, study, research of PARTICULAR subject or cause and their mind generates fresh energy that keeps them fit and alive.

Passionate people's mind support them like camel's multi-functional stomach in the desert. Their hunger is very strong, that makes them passionate in comparison to others.

2. Happiness

They know very well how to remain POSITIVE and happy all the time in any of the situation because they are prepared for any failure. Can a sad guy create innovative solution from his mind…NEVER. All innovations come from bloody fresh mind. Here "bloody" means full of "fresh blood" in their brain. Bloody Happy…ha ha ;)

3. Energy. Full of Power

They have more than enough energy, EXTRA power, that is required to accomplish any bigger task. Rejections, refusals have opposite impact in their mind, that's HARD-WORK.

They have extra energy to work hard. Examples, they can talk and…. talk about their ideas and business more than an hour without taking a pause.

Remember first point, what are their energy supplies –
fresh and strong mind ;)

4. Stubborn. They believe in themselves

They believe in themselves and look like stubborn on specific research or innovation. Even if their knowledge for PARTICULAR subject has made them rich, people don't see it clearly, until somebody INVEST into them and make money. Example of Henry Ford proves this point, the owner of the Ford Motor Company, whose automobile revolutionized transportation and became one of the richest man. (Source: Wiki - Henry Ford).

5. They Never Quit

Yes, their mind has many options which nobody have even thought of yet and they keep trying one by one before all expired and failed and then they come up with NEW LIST of options from their mind. They keep producing possibilities…ha ha ;) They are never tired. They never quit.

6. Leadership

They have inborn qualities to lead everybody around them. They teach and lead the World.

Can you become passionate?

This is still debatable question that whether passion is inborn or can be taught by motivating people to chase their dreams. I think that is possible if they are guided well to search ANSWER within themselves what they want from their life.

Passion also germinates from the past life events, like Steve Jobs has different past life which might have impacted to be passionate to show the world what he has created. Everybody's life has some events that trigger their mind to follow their dreams and be passionate.

#STARTUPS

*"Profitability is a playground where **#startups** business can play. Build it"*

Great start-ups NEVER started with thinking profitability at first, but with a motive to contribute VALUE to their customers, society. Great value, great business. Simple.

But it is very often, start-ups forget Profitability.

Here are the reasons why entrepreneurs don't focus much on profitability in the INITIAL days and forget sometime even later.

1. **Great Entrepreneurs focus on value**

They have no ability to see MONEY MONEY MONEY everywhere. They focus on creating VALUE first. They are blind. Sitting on the pile of money, but they never realize it, until somebody outsiders (investors) knock knock knock their doors which sounds like valuation, valuation, valuation.

2. **They are driven by passion**

Their Love for work or vision never makes money as priority and creates illusion of growth without making money.

I sometime meet entrepreneurs to mentor them and every time I ask them how much margin they are earning, they behave like I have asked some odd question. They are happy with customers loving them and some are only happy with website traffic…..ha ha ;)

3. **They are easily amused by their fame**

They become popular and feel cheap if they expect money from their fans. They are loyal to their fans.

4. **They think they are alone. Emotional driven people**

In every struggle in early days, they find nobody supportive. Their family and friends. Even if they are responsible themselves for the same.

Now things are evolving. Technology is giving more OPPORTUNITIES. Now entrepreneur must realize following things.

1. **Profitability is a playground**

If you are hand to mouth in cash flow, how come you can invest into GROWTH or any INNOVATION. Every time start-up has cash flow problem because majority of the income goes to operations and giving salaries to employees.

Just imagine, business is a game and profitability is a ground.

The more space of playground, the more comfortable for your play. Similarly, if your business has more profitability, you will invest into GROWTH. Growth means investment into things like marketing, research, innovation, technology, which will generate more profit.

Build a large playground and play your game, means business.

2. **Try to Play Safe**

Entrepreneur never play safe anything, that is why they are entrepreneur. Please try ;) You can't expect profitability from something without creating HUGE VALUE for customers.

Keep adding value so that your customers can pay you HIGHER price of the same product or service even if your competitor is selling it cheap. Customer will pay you more if there is BIGGER value differentiation.

In my case, my company has been selling different price memberships to same customer by adding value into it. We started with memberships selling and today we are selling it at little higher price, and customer still pay because we have added more VALUE to it.

3. **Spend Less. EARN MORE**

This is business rule and you forget every time. You must know your strength. The Founder has to contribute 70% of his knowledge and skills to start-up and rest can be hired. All entrepreneurs think to HIRE for every function in the initial days before they realized later when they run out of cash.

There is no perfect formula of Optimal Performance of staff. So, just find ways to get work done by existing staff than hiring more people to bring profitability.

4. **Pay Yourself First**

It has been seen that when you start business and you don't try to pay yourself first. I understand you are loyal to your team and want salary at the last. Your team is loyal and working hard. Tell me one thing. Who is the person who will never leave your company and remain LOYAL to your company......YOU.... You deserve paying yourself first. If you pay yourself FIRST, you can help anybody with savings if somebody is in need later or you are in any cash-crunch situation. I can tell you how many intelligent people I have lost just because I had no money to help them and help myself too. In my case, I had no playground how I can pay. Investors don't build the playground, they just want you to win the game ;)

Build Playground. Be Profitable.
Lets PLAY business ;)

✳ ✳ ✳ ✳ ✳

#SUCCCESS

"Get Rejected.

Fail FAST

for

*Big **#Success**"*

Every successful person failed at least once before making it a big success. If this is true, then you have to fail FAST so that you can meet your SUCCESS early in your life.

How Rejections or Failing can help you.

1. The REAL world means – CHALLENGES

The real world is when you get challenged and you try again and again and become successful. Human mind is STUBBORN; we try what we are not allowed to. Recall the evolution of human from monkey in the history. Today monkeys are all those who did NOT try to evolve into human and were lazy.

So try something NEW, get challenges and your success will be an output of your "challenged evolution" and don't be monkey…ha ha ;) Be Fast.

2. Failing is great learning than just reading books

How many times we read in the books, CASH is KING, we got to know its real MEANING when we had pain living without cash. Most of start ups, ventures run out of cash in early days and are closed down.

If you think that by reading manuals, training material and motivational books and academic books and success love stories, novels can make you LEARN. Not at all. Readings are OPTIONS, paths, DIRECTIONS you may or may not required.

Reading has less impact on mind than "doing" but failing has GREATER IMPACT, it releases real human emotions, it releases real hormones in the body, you probably can't forget even in the NEXT LIFE. Yeah, NEXT life…ha ha ;)

See how you can't forget PAIN of failure and try hard to overcome, to WIN. Emotions give more strength and courage to WIN. You have to "do", "try", "fail" and then " learn" and see what you have gained with experience. SUCCESS. Experience it.

Experience makes the difference

Reading can give you KNOWLEDGE, options, experience can give you SUCCESS. Just do it.

3. **Rejections help to find MORE BETTER options**

Sitting at home thinking somebody will reject you, you have already invited FEAR around you. You have already wasted lot of time thinking it. Get up, get rejected so that you can try another option or you will be wasting time on ONE option. There are many opportunities, you have to move fast. Keep trying. Knocking the doors of opportunities. One and only one opportunity is waiting to make you successful.

In my office, there was one sales executive who was lazy doing follow ups because he always thought client never pick up his call…ha ha ;)

Fear of rejection is the biggest hurdle in human life for success.

Win over it.

* * * * *

Opportunity is waiting for you and you have not started yet. START now.

* * * * *

#HESITATION

"#Hesitation

is a closed door

in your mind.

Only positiveness

can OPEN it"

Why we all have these hesitations? These are barriers to check, or small "tests" to pass through before you achieve GREAT things. Now the major problem is how to win over and come out without hesitation. Dare and courage is required to win over hesitation. Only positive vibes and energy can help to push the door of hesitation and you come out a free soul with no more hesitations.

Here is a list of some of the very common hesitations

1. Hesitation when you ask for a HELP

Majority of people hesitate to ask for help. The biggest problem is when you do not know if you need help. I offered many people help, but they never revert back for asking help even. Our ego also plays a major role. You are forgetting you are NOT perfect. Here are some questions come into mind when asking for a help:

- You think that they don't have time.

- You think that why they will help me.

Honestly, we do not trust people.

There are people who really help others until they do not loose anything in returns. Just ask nicely even if the answer is "No". Think if they really help, you save your time or money or anything you wanted.

2. Fear of Rejections

When you get rejected, mood is so low, you are sad that you need courage to do it again next time. Fear of rejections creates so many hesitations. Mind stops working. Think if it gets accepted, the job offer, the marriage proposal, the salary hike, then you are at the top. Get up and Just do it now.

In my experience, I always got something when I did it without hesitation and fear. I dare to start a company when nobody believed me. I dare to reach to top investors and got their investments for my company. I win over fear and hesitation.

3. When you want to say – I Love You

This is very common in young age when you start liking somebody (opposite) and mind has much confusion. All confusions creates so much barrier that you can't speak THREE words...ha ha ;) The most of the reasons of not saying are what has no meaning at all.

4. Hesitation to appreciate or giving credit

In professional life, not appreciating people and not giving credit to others for what you get from others help is another form of hesitation. When you appreciate others, you are not only making others happy, but yourself too.

Here are some safety tips:

Just TRY without thinking that you will be fired, half job is already done, the only thing left is to "Be SPECIFIC".

Hesitations are form of negative thoughts which prevent you to win over it, so make a list of positive thoughts. That power of positive-ness will help you. Try to win over ;)

Start thinking POSITIVE
and come out of hesitations.

* * * *

#SUCCESS

"Speed is

the key

*to #**success**"*

Everybody's life is changing, evolving and transforming and becoming COMPLEX. You have many things to achieve in your life. Many expectations.

Technology has made things simple but mind is still occupied with many things. There is more competitive environment because everybody is running for the same goal.

You have NOT started yet. You are slow in your life. You have many reasons to prove that why you are slow. Here are some of those excuses:

1. You think your circumstances are not good.
2. You still need more experience to start.
3. You have to finish academic qualification.
4. You think you should be little older.
5. You have not much information.
6. You don't get much time.

All above reasons are EXCUSES. It is all created by yourself to keep you in doubt all the time. How you can be FAST. Just follow this quickly:

1. Networking
Join all groups, social media and networking websites and contact like minded and experienced people to get subject knowledge.

2. Meet people
You have to go and get appointment and visit people.

3. Get mentor
Great mentors are those who are NOT from your domain, but have life experience of running businesses, career or subject.

Be fast. Speed is the key ;)

#VISION

"Glimpse of success makes you run faster.

*Create **#vision**"*

It is normal when you see something reaching its completion, you would try to finish it fast. Assume you are a sports person and you are close to finish line. You would have more energy and run faster at that moment to reach destination. Similarly, we all have our goal of life, but keep doing it slowly and considering we have enough time is actually laziness.

Here, glimpse means, realizing small successes and destination means your life goal and you have to achieve it fast.

At the age of 20, you say I am still young and have enough time. At 27, you say, lets get married I have just started my life, at 35 I am enjoying and let me have some more years of experience. At 45, let me think what I should do. You are at 50 now, your main task is this – smiling on other's goal ;)

Make your goals. Small successes will make you confident. Achieve it FAST.

Once I participated in the business plan competition and got selected. One younger contestant asked me – what is your age? I laughed and asked why. His reply surprised me when he said I am still young and have enough time to achieve at your age (pointed out towards me). We all think like the same.

Who has enough time? You? Not at all. Why don't you do it now? Finish what you want to do and enjoy your life.

How can you see your life journey, path and destination when you have NOT started yet?

How you can be successful fast. Here are few guidelines:

1. Create Vision. Life Goals

You must decide quickly what you want to achieve in your life. Talk to people. Get advice from industry people. Decide what you want to be.

2. Glimpse of destination

When you know what is your goal. Start putting in small efforts. Every success of small efforts will give you an idea how much time you will take to reach your ultimate goal. For example, you want to create an online shop. Registering a domain name and checking later if somebody has filled up contact form is small success. Validation. It is glimpse of your goal. If few visitors come to your website, it means, you can make more people to visit. You are on the right path. It's glimpse of destination.

Another example, you want to be professional painter. Do some efforts to arrange a small event in your colony displaying all your paintings, this is small success. Similarly, join dance group, yoga classes. Do it now.

Enjoy your journey ;)

* * * *

#ACCEPT-YOURSELF

"Do not try hard to change yourself.

#*Accept* *Yourself*"

Knowing yourself means knowing STRENGTH and weaknesses and then accept yourself "as it is". Be successful.

You can only improve (change) those things which you have acquired, but you have to accept what you are "born with"– Qualities which are inborn.

If you are creative by birth, you remain creative. Acceptance means awareness about yourself. If you are trying hard to become somebody else, you are really trying to FAIL yourself.

If you think you can be a great a dancer, a writer, an artist, a painter. You should try to do the same.

If you think you have great qualities of managing people, team building, then you should try to make career in that.

If you are lazy, then be lazy. You will surely find way to do something for yourself. Did you know many companies hire lazy because their SYSTEMS are very smart. They have made Robots. You have a job there. Mr. Lazy…ha ha;)

If you are creative, CREATE something.
If you are innovative, INNOVATE something.
If you are passionate, create VALUES.
If you are manager, MANAGE the world.
Here is a list to tell you why you should accept yourself.

1. You are different and unique

Everybody has their own life path. Nobody's life events matches others. You can get inspired from anybody. But you can only rely on your own capabilities. Only your siblings can have similarities and somewhat same life path.

2. You have one strong strength

Probably, you might have not realized yet, there are qualities and capabilities which you can do better than anybody else. It is always confusion until you TRY all. Narrow down to your one strength. Results will help you.

3. Your Past Life has some hidden hints

Many times, parents watch and see their kids doing something great in one field or subject and motivate for the same. That past events may tell you what kind of professional life you can make.

Search within. Know Yourself ;)

✳ ✳ ✳ ✳

#ENTREPRENEUR

"An Entrepreneur

Is a Teacher.

They teach the World"

An Entrepreneur is a teacher who builds his vision of life around people. They teach everything they learn from their journey.

Their ideas, their vision, their money and everything they think, they have people in their mind. When they have ideas, they talk to people to validate their ideas and know if that can benefit people. When they have vision, they spread awareness about future trends. When they need money, they pitch their ideas to tell how their ideas can bring more money to investors.

They TEACH the world – that's YOU ;)

Why Entrepreneurs are The Best Teacher,

Here are the reasons:

1. They Believe in Themselves

You can not learn from people who are in doubts. Never. You can only learn from people who believe in themselves. They are never be in doubts of what they are building. They try many different routes to achieve what they believe in. They keep innovating.

2. They are Not Shy telling you their MISTAKES

They laugh and enjoy while telling you their mistakes. Why they do this? They want you not to try or be cautious of doing the same mistakes. They never feel bad sharing their failure stories, because they want YOU to learn from them.

3. They always spread happiness

Happiness and joy are food for their mind. They enjoy their own journey and spread awareness about the values of life. Sometimes even if you have enough money, you still lack something, that's happiness.

4. They really know the value of Love

They know very well about that pain when society rejected their beliefs, they know when their own loved ones tried to stop them not to follow their dreams. Do they get over all the past stuffs when they are successful? Yes. They spread and teach the value of love. They teach others not to loose people they love.

Be Entrepreneur. Be Teacher ;)

✲ ✲ ✲ ✲

#PEOPLE

*"#Success is -

right TIME, right

PEOPLE

& right MONEY.

Just ensure RIGHT

people & wait for rest."*

If Success is right TIME, right MONEY and right PEOPLE, then get the right PEOPLE first and other two things will come to you automatically to make you SUCCESSFUL.

Now the problem is how to find the RIGHT people.

Here is the list.

1. Who educate you

If you don't have KNOWLEDGE, you are already dead. There is no success without knowledge. You need to appreciate who educate you.

2. Who screw you when you do mistakes

Don't get disheartened. They are CRITICS. Finding the right Critics is another job, otherwise there are many free critics roaming around.

3. Who promotes you. Your Fans.

People who talks about YOU before others, who feel proud of being connected with you, know you very well. They help you to bring your FIRST customer or promote your startup and help you in networking.

4. Who invests in you

Who are investing their money, time and energy for their own betterment. If you don't win, they also don't win. Parents? Girl/Boy friend? Close Family? Feeling proud is the only expectation of parents and they spend their entire life making you a MAN. Count Investors also with lots money too ;) Their only interest is – making money from your effort. You will work hard, they get their money multiplied, you both get money.

5. Who follow you

Your team, staffs, juniors who follow you to help you to meet your VISION. I call them "Wish Team". You have a vision, but you can't do things alone. You need a team who just fulfill your "wishes". They are the only one that can make you success or failure. In startups, they are the first one to eat your money, time and energy. Most of the startups shut down just because they hired wrong people. Choose them carefully.

6. Who is available for you anytime

They are caring people on the earth. OMG, God has given them EXTRA ENERGY. They always have time for you. Even if you feel they are free all the time, actually they make themselves available free for you. Pray God that they become successful before you, because if they are successful, you don't need anybody else from the above list. They are actually well-wishers. Mentors also come into this category, but they are also of different types. Find.

7. Your Emotional Friends on this earth ;) The people who Love you

The people who love you. They like you, pampers you and even understand your silence…yeah there are people who try to understand you. How come I got a call asking "are you ok?" when I am expecting. Telepathy? They meet your emotional needs of being connected mentally. Human is social animal.

If you do not find anybody the right people, write to me at **contact@rakeshsidana.org** and make me your friend. I may help you ;)

You already got everything once you have right PEOPLE.

About The Author

Rakesh Sidana is Founder and CEO of MeriCAR.com. He has been known by his passion and persistence for building Unique and Unusual business for Car Aftermarket in India. He started his career in 1997 and established his own consultancy in 2004 after working with reputed dot com companies in India.

He worked with international clients all across the world before launching India Project. He has been recognized in the industry, media and appeared on TV shows for his entrepreneurship driven business.

At the age of over 40, he is sharing his experiences and he loves to motivate students, entrepreneurs and startups with his positive thoughts. This book is supported and sponsored by his company.

He wants to contribute to NGO by selling the hardcover of this book. You can read more about him on his website **http://www.rakeshsidana.org** and connect him on facebook for daily thoughts at: **http://www.facebook.com/rakesh.sidana**

RakeshSidana.ORG

This is not-for-profit organization website formed dedicated to helping underprivileged kids. We are committed to helping children reach their full potential by educating them through a school.

If you have bought this book from direct source (rakeshsidana.ORG), then you have already contributed to donation. Thanks for buying hardcover version.

Even eBook is still free with some chapters, but we have kept some chapters in the hardcover book for the purpose of generating donation through this book.

Please contact and visit us online:

Facebook:

https://www.facebook.com/iwanttoflywherearemywings

YouTube TV:

http://www.youtube.com/channel/UC471il-kBAu-E80dUij7cCQ

Google Plus:

https://plus.google.com/105421917652961851347/

Email: contact@rakeshsidana.org

GMail: iwanttofly.wherearemywings@gmail.com

MY LAST WORDS IN A #POEM

I am your source

a source from where positive energy
comes out to kill negative energy.

a source from where love and wish
comes out to make hate and jealousy finish.

a source from where knowledge spreads
and brings out awareness.

a source from where technology enable
people to be comfortable.

a source from where happiness grows
and sadness forever goes.

a source from where everybody become successful
and life become joyful.

a source from where you WIN
and make me WIN

I am your source from where
You win
I win.

- Rakesh Sidana

FEEDBACK / TESTIMONIAL FORM

Dear Readers,

Thanks for reading this book. We would like to know about your feedback about this book. How did you find this book useful? This is Rakesh Sidana's First Book. Any message to him will be appreciated. Thank You! NOTE: This information will be personal for Rakesh Sidana just for his book feedback and will NEVER used for any other purpose.

Name:_____

Mobile_____Email_____

Your Message to Rakesh Sidana

_____

_____

_____

_____

NOTE: Please tear this page & Post this form at:
Rakesh Sidana, Amoeba Webware Pvt Ltd, Vatika Triangle, 2nd Floor, M.G. Road, Gurgaon, Haryana, India – Pin: 122002
Or Write an Email:
contact@rakeshsidana.ORG
http://www.rakeshsidana.org

www.ingramcontent.com/pod-product-compliance
Lightning Source LLC
Chambersburg PA
CBHW071757170526
45167CB00003B/1061